Exploring
NORTHEASTERN AMERICA

Rose Blue and Corinne J. Naden

Raintree
Chicago, Illinois

© 2003 Raintree
Published by Raintree,
a division of Reed Elsevier, Inc.
Chicago, Illinois
Customer Service 888-454-2279
Visit our website at www.raintreelibrary.com

Printed and bound in the United States.

07 06 05 04 03
10 9 8 7 6 5 4 3 2 1

Library of Congress Cataloging-in-Publication Data:

Blue, Rose.
   Exploring northeastern America / Rose Blue and Corinne J. Naden.
      v. cm. -- (Exploring the Americas)
Includes bibliographical references (p.) and index.
Contents: Prologue: who found it? -- Leif Ericson: in the days of the Vikings (c. 1000) -- John Cabot: changing the map of Canada (1496-98) -- Giovanni da Verrazano: mapping the east coast (1524-28) -- Martin Frobisher: looking for the passage west (1576-78) -- Humphrey Gilbert and the almost colony (1578-83) -- John Davis: a path through the Arctic (1585-87) -- Henry Hudson and the four voyages (1607-11) -- Epilogue: what did they find? -- Important events in the exploration of northeastern America -- Major dates in the search for the Northwest Passage.
   ISBN 0-7398-4948-4 (HC), 1-4109-0042-8 (Pbk.)
   1. Northeastern States--Discovery and exploration--Juvenile literature. 2. Explorers--Northeastern States--Biography--Juvenile literature. 3. Canada, Eastern--Discovery and exploration--Juvenile literature. 4. Explorers--Canada, Eastern--Biography--Juvenile literature. [1. Northeastern States--Discovery and exploration. 2. Canada, Eastern--Discovery and exploration. 3. Explorers.] I. Naden, Corinne J. II. Title.
F106 .B655 2003
974'.01--dc21
                                   2002013353

Acknowledgments
The author and publishers are grateful to the following for permission to reproduce copyright material:

Cover photographs by SuperStock, (map) Corbis

p. 4 Christie's Images/SuperStock; p. 6 Lee Snider/Corbis; pp. 7, 12, 18, 20, 35, 46, 50, 58 Bettmann/Corbis; p. 9 Wolfgang Kaehler/Corbis; p. 10 Tim Thompson/Corbis; p. 15 John Farmar/Cordaiy Photo Library Ltd./Corbis; p. 16 Paul A. Souders/Corbis; p. 21 Charles E. Rotkin/Corbis; p. 23 Kevin Fleming/Corbis; p. 24 Vince Streano/Corbis; pp. 26, 36, 41, 48 Hulton Archive/Getty Images; pp. 28, 54 Archivo Iconografico, S. A./Corbis; p. 30 Gordon Miller; p. 32 Alison Wright/Corbis; p. 34 Kennan Ward/Corbis; p. 39 Lowell Georgia/Corbis; p. 40 Pierre Perrin/Corbis SYGMA; p. 42 National Library of Canada; p. 44 Kevin Schafer/Corbis; p. 47 Hubert Stadler/Corbis

Photo research by Alyx Kellington

Some words are shown in bold, like **this.** You can find out what they mean by looking in the Glossary.

Contents

Prologue:

Who Found It?

Who found it? Somebody claimed to be the first to see all the places we know by name. Sometimes we call that *somebody* an explorer. We say that explorers discovered things and places, but do we really mean "discovered"? Had these explorers gone where no one else had gone before? In most cases, no. Generally, native peoples were living in the areas that the explorers discovered.

Explorers may not have been the first to see places, but they were usually the first to talk or write about them. The very word "explorer" sounds like excitement, danger, or a step into the unknown. Astronauts are explorers who step into the unknown of outer space, just as the explorers in this book stepped into the unknown of northeastern America. When they sailed from Europe, these adventurers had no idea that two continents lay across the Atlantic Ocean.

Who were these early explorers? Certainly they must have been ambitious and brave people, possibly reckless and even greedy. Most of all, they were curious. What is behind that mountain? Where does that river go? Is the earth round even though it looks flat? Will my ship drop off the world if I sail beyond the horizon? Strange as it may sound, until the mid-1500s, most people believed that the earth was flat. If you got to the end of the earth, you might drop off.

An early map shows how Europeans first pictured the New World.

The early explorers in this book were among the many adventurers from Europe who sailed to the so-called New World. It would later be named North and South America. Why are these explorers so important? Because, for better or for worse, they changed the world as it was recorded until that time. They may not have been the first to see a certain site, but they were the first to examine, describe, and map regions of the world that Europeans never knew existed. They gave European names to the places and things they "discovered." They laid the groundwork for all the colonists, adventurers, and fortune seekers who would follow them.

This book tells the story of seven explorers who first put northeastern America—parts of the United States and Canada—on the map. It is the story of Henry Hudson, Leif Ericson and John Cabot, Giovanni da Verrazano, Martin Frobisher, Humphrey Gilbert, and John Davis. Christopher Columbus is not included in this story. Even though he gets the credit for discovering the Americas, he never reached the northeastern coast. Neither did Amerigo Vespucci, the man for whom the New World continents are named.

Why did the people in this book go exploring? Why did all those voyages take place from about the year 1000 to Hudson's last voyage in 1611? During those centuries, there was no telephone, no radar, no sonar, and certainly no computers. In fact, there was no electricity at all. There were no maps of the area, no nautical charts of the Atlantic coast, and no reliable weather forecasts.

These adventurers were really sailing into the unknown. All they had were their ships, rowed by men or blown by the wind. Leif Ericson's longships carried oarsmen in addition to sails. By Hudson's time, sails were the way to go. The steamship would not make an appearance until the mid-1800s.

Why would anyone go on a journey that was so dangerous? Why would anyone go to the moon? Some people say that adventurers go after something because "it is there," such as climbing to the top of Mt. Everest. But in these cases, the explorers did not know that anything was there.

All kinds of reasons sent each of these explorers sailing west. The chance of finding gold and other riches was a good reason to explore. So were fame and duty to the flag under which each sailed. But there was a practical reason to sail across the Atlantic Ocean. Many adventurers were looking for the Northwest Passage. Each European power wanted to be the first to find a water route around or through this new land so they could sail straight to the Far East. It would mean a great saving in time and money compared to overland trade routes or sailing around the tip of Africa. The search would occupy Europe for hundreds of years.

This story of exploration includes hair-raising journeys and colorful people. It talks of bravery and frightening superstitions. It tells how a whole new world, roughly the region from northern Canada to southern New York State, was uncovered. It begins with the daring voyages of the Viking, Leif Ericson. It ends with an explorer for whom so many present-day places are named: the mysterious English **navigator** Henry Hudson.

Chapter One
Leif Ericson
In the Days of the Vikings (c.1000)

I f ever a person was born to explore, it was probably Leif Ericson, known as Leif the Lucky (c. 970–?). He could trace his seafaring ancestors through a long line of Vikings from Denmark, Norway, and Sweden. They were also known as Norsemen or Northmen or even Norse Sea Kings. Viking warriors were the terror of Europe for more than 200 years, until about the year 1050.

The small island of Lindisfarne off England's northeastern coast is a good example of Viking power centuries ago. The small island in the North Sea held a church and monastery dating from about the year 635. One bright morning in 793, the monks spotted ships with great square sails and dragon heads on the **prow** coming over the horizon. Before they could think to react or even realize that they should be terrified, the ships had landed on the island shore. With piercing screams, hordes of red-blond men streamed from the ships, swinging swords and axes above their heads. Monks, servants, and women were struck down without mercy or tied up and captured. Others were taken out to sea and drowned.

When the Viking invaders left Lindisfarne—now known as Holy Island — a short time later, it was on fire and in ruins. The destruction was terrible and complete, and it occurred again and again in northern Europe. There was no

A statue of Leif Ericson (c.970–?)

defense from these well-trained, brutal warriors.

Who were these feared Vikings? They were pagans from Scandinavia who probably began their raids for two reasons: overpopulation in their own lands and the fact that success was so easy for them. In England the raids began in earnest about 865, and in a few years much of the North was in Viking hands. But Alfred the Great of Wessex proved a worthy foe and forced a treaty with the Vikings in about 886, which left much of England in Danish hands. It took until 954 for the territory to be returned to England. Viking warriors were no longer a threat by the mid-11th century during the reign of William I.

Ireland recorded Viking invasions starting in about 795. They raided France up and down the Atlantic coast, but never on the scale on which they invaded the British Isles.

The Vikings were not only warriors, but farmers, explorers, traders, and settlers as well. Even more than fighting, perhaps, they had a restless urge to move on. Their heroic poems, called **sagas,** tell of this constant search for new places and more freedom. In fact, most of what we know about the Vikings comes from these sagas, or "tellings," handed down through the centuries.

Ericson's family as exiles

Leif Ericson himself was born in Iceland, an island in the North Atlantic between Norway and Greenland, about the year 970. His father was Eric Thorvaldsson (son of Thorvald), known as Eric the Red. About the year 960, Eric's father was thrown out of his native Norway for killing a neighbor. The family was allowed to settle in the north of Iceland. When Eric was grown and married, in about the year 982, he, too, killed a neighbor— actually, two sons of a neighbor— over a dispute. For that crime, he was sent into exile for three years.

Eric the Red sailed to Greenland, about 175 miles (282 kilometers) to the west of Iceland. He and his family, which now included Leif, were the first Europeans to settle on that island, the world's largest. Now part of Denmark, Greenland lies across the Davis **Strait** from northern Canada. The name, which Eric may have chosen to entice settlers, is misleading. Rather than a place of green, the island's 840,000 square miles (2,175,590

A drawing depicts Leif Ericson's father, Eric the Red, in full armor.

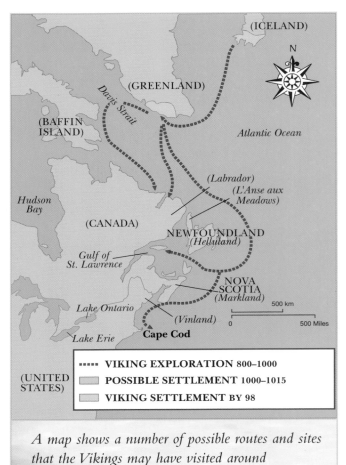

A map shows a number of possible routes and sites that the Vikings may have visited around 1000–1015.

Map legend:
- **VIKING EXPLORATION 800–1000**
- **POSSIBLE SETTLEMENT 1000–1015**
- **VIKING SETTLEMENT BY 98**

square kilometers) are mostly covered with ice. But the advertising must have worked, because Eric lured several hundred settlers in 985 and became a sort of king in the barren land.

In about the year 1000, Leif Ericson left Greenland and sailed to Norway, where King Olaf I converted him to Christianity. At the king's urging, Ericson sailed home a year later to acquaint the settlers with his new religion. But on the way, according to most records, he sailed off course.

Navigating the high seas in Leif Ericson's time was a world away from the way it is done today. Although Viking ships were very seaworthy and Viking sailors very skilled, a long sea voyage was not for the faint of heart or weak of stomach. Constantly exposed to the sea and outside temperatures, the sailors were usually wet and cold at all times. They slept in bags, wearing as much woolen clothing—usually wet—as they could put on. No cooking fires were allowed on board, of course, so they ate salted fish and bacon plus whatever they could catch at sea. If a storm blew a ship off course, the crew's limited water supplies might run out before it reached land. Not surprisingly, one of the most important of the Viking gods was Aegir, god of the sea.

Ericson landed on the North American continent in a place of fertile soil and wild grapes. He called it Vinland. It might have been Nova Scotia, across the **Bay** of Fundy from New Brunswick, Canada, and Maine. It might have been Labrador or New-foundland, or even farther south. Some scholars argue that it was Newfoundland because of the wild grapes, known to have been growing in Newfoundland until the mid-1600s.

Wherever it was, Ericson had already heard of it. About fourteen years earlier, Icelander Bjarni Herjulfsson had appar-

The village of Angmagssalik in Greenland lies just below the Arctic Circle.

ently seen a strange new land when he was thrown off course while trying to reach Greenland. When he got home, he said the land seemed to have good timber and a warmer climate. Young Leif had heard the tales of this new place and decided he had found it.

Ericson and his crew spent some time exploring the country, where apparently no one else was living. They cut timber and harvested grapes. On the trip back to Greenland, loaded with timber and other goods, Ericson rescued a stranded ship and took on more trade goods. For this successful voyage, he got the name of Leif the Lucky.

That is one story. But not all scholars believe it. It is very difficult to find out exactly what happened so many centuries ago. No one kept records, certainly none that survived. But from a few clues, some believe that Ericson was not blown off course to the American mainland. They say his voyage was intentional. He had heard Herjulfsson's tales of a hilly, forested land west of Greenland. Always seeking new farmland and with the urge to discover in his blood, Ericson set out to find this place.

If this version of the trip is true, Ericson followed Herjulfsson's voyage in reverse and made three landings.

This reconstructed sod home at L'Anse Aux Meadows Historical park in Canada shows the way Vikings once lived.

The first he named Helluland, which means "flat stone." This landing was probably Labrador. The second he called Markland, meaning "wood land." The location of the third, which he named Vinland, is less certain. Some guess it was in Nova Scotia or as far south as Cape Cod in Massachusetts. Possibly, it was even farther north in Newfoundland. Early evidence for the location of Vinland is too vague to locate it with any accuracy. Wherever it was, Ericson and his crew spent the winter there before returning to Greenland.

If Ericson had already heard of this new place from Herjulfsson, why does Leif the Lucky get credit for being first? Because Herjulfsson only saw the land from his ship and never actually landed on it. Ericson, as far as we know, was the first European to actually set foot in America. However, he never went back.

Some time after Ericson returned home, his father died. About a year later, Ericson's brother Thorvald decided to set sail to explore Vinland. He outfitted a ship and returned to the site of his brother's landing. We know little about the voyage except that Thorvald was wounded in a fight with native peoples. He died and was buried there. In about the year 1006, another brother, Thorstein, might have attempted an expedition to Vinland but was blown off course in bad weather and never reached his destination. These Viking explorers from Greenland never made permanent settlements on the North American continent. An ambitious venture was started in 1011 by Icelander Thorfinn Karlsefni. He took about 100 settlers to the new land in the hope of starting a new colony. Although they attempted to trade with the native peoples, fighting broke out and drove the would-be colonists back to Greenland within two years. The last attempt at a colony was attempted by Leif's half-sister Freydis, but that also ended in war between native peoples and newcomers.

Information from Icelandic **sagas** has led scholars to believe that Leif Ericson and other Vikings did land somewhere in the New World, although the exact spot remains a mystery. Actual remains of such expeditions are hard to find.

A number of **artifacts** have been uncovered through the years, but none has proved authentic. In the 1960s, Helge Ingstad published a book called *Land Under the Pole Star*. In it, he writes of his archaeological research and his reasons for believing that Leif Ericson landed in Newfoundland. Excavations did uncover what are thought to be the sites of very, very old houses, and some of the findings seem to agree with the small amount of data taken from the Viking sagas of the time. But does that mean for certain that Leif Ericson was there? Or are the ruins the remains of the colony attempted by Karlsefni's group? There are no sure answers to these questions.

Greenlanders often argue that Christopher Columbus should not be hailed as the European who "discovered" the North American continent. After all, they say, a Viking got there 500 years earlier. Ancient records being what they are, Leif the Lucky has had to take second place to the Italian explorer. However, in 1964, at last the Viking received a little more recognition. President Lyndon B. Johnson proclaimed October 9 as Leif Ericson Day.

Chapter Two
John Cabot
Changing the Map of Canada (1496–1498)

The story of John Cabot (1450–1499) is quite amazing. Considering how little we know about him, it is amazing how his name pops up in so many places in Canada. Periodically, Newfoundland, Canada, goes into a sort of Cabot fever. In June 1997 Bonavista, Newfoundland, a little fishing village of about 4,500 people, celebrated the 500th anniversary of Cabot's landing. A replica of Cabot's ship, the *Mathew,* sailed into town all the way from Bristol, England. About 70 small boats floated down the St. Lawrence River for the celebration. When the *Mathew* came into view on June 24, Queen Elizabeth II of England was there to greet it. She said that Newfoundland had been a link between the old and new worlds. Even the weather seemed to cooperate in Newfoundland fashion. The festivities went on in a light drizzle, although the sun did come out the following morning. By then, no one was around to take pictures. However, as one onlooker said, "If it had been balmy, it would have been just another day."

It did not seem to bother anybody at the celebration, including the queen, that scholars do not know for sure where Cabot actually landed. No one is certain that he landed in Bonavista on June 24 or any other day, or that he landed in Newfoundland at all. Cabot fever was in full swing. And not only in Bonavista.

A portrait of John Cabot (1450–1499)

Look at a map of Canada and you will surely find evidence of Cabot fever. Cabot **Strait** separates southwestern Newfoundland from Cape Breton Island. Labrador has Cabot Lake. Cabot Head is a little piece of land on the end of Bruce Peninsula in Ontario. It has the Cabot Head lighthouse, built in 1896, to guide ships leaving and entering Lake Huron. Some say the capital of Newfoundland, St. John's, also honors the explorer—if one believes that he landed there on June 24, 1497, the feast of St. John the Baptist. The United States even got into the Cabot swing. The fictional fishing village of Cabot Cove, Maine, was the setting for the television show "Murder, She Wrote," starring Angela Lansbury as detective and writer Jessica Fletcher. This show was highly popular from 1984 through the mid-1990s.

John Cabot is also credited by some with a less noble distinction. A tribe of Native Americans known as Boethuk and numbering about 500 once lived in Newfoundland. Supposedly Cabot met them in 1497. It was their religious practice to smear red ochre on their skins. It might have been used as protection against insects. Cabot is said to have called them "redskins," a name used to refer to Native Americans until the mid-20th century. By about 1830, the Boethuks of Newfoundland were wiped out, having been killed by the European newcomers or fallen victim to European diseases. This did not go unnoticed during the Cabot celebration in Bonavista in 1997. A group of pro-Boethuk protesters beat drums and held signs during the parade.

The unknown about Cabot

Even with all the names on maps, historians and mapmakers are still arguing about John Cabot. What do we know? His real name was Giovanni Caboto. He was probably born in Genoa, Italy, probably around the year 1450. But he sailed under the British flag and we know him by his English name. Most details about his life are uncertain. However, he is said to be the first European to set foot on the North American mainland since Leif Ericson and the Vikings did so some centuries earlier.

Sometime in the 1460s or later, Cabot went to Venice. His wife was a Venetian named Mattea. Cabot became a citizen of the city in 1476. At the time, Venice was the major trading center for all of the Mediterranean, a focal point for the exchange of Western and Eastern goods. Cabot worked as a **merchant** and became skilled as a **navigator,** making short trips to eastern Mediterranean ports.

It is thought that Cabot was living in the Spanish city of Valencia in 1493. If so, he may have seen Christopher Columbus as he passed through the city on his way to report to the king and queen of Spain about his successful journey to the New World in 1492.

Even if he did not see Columbus, Cabot had certainly heard the exciting news. However, many believed that Columbus had not discovered anything new. They thought he had just found a different way to Asia. But Cabot disagreed. He reasoned that Asia must be farther away than the distance Columbus traveled. Cabot thought that Columbus might have found a new world. He also thought it might be possible to get around it and reach Asia that way. Thus began the search for the Northwest Passage. This quest to find a quicker way to the Far East would prompt many, many voyages over the next 300 years.

New theories, old fears

It is difficult for someone living in the 21st century to visualize how people in the 1500s and 1600s saw the world around them. Today, we talk about sending people to other planets. But in 1543, Polish astronomer Nicolaus Copernicus stunned everyone just by saying that Earth revolved around the Sun, not the other way around. Some years later, Italian Giordano Bruno took it a step further. He said that our universe could contain many worlds and an infinite number of stars. This so incensed the established churches that Bruno was burned at the stake. Italian mathematician Galileo ran into a lot of trouble with the church, too. He supported the idea that Earth revolves around the Sun. For that, he was under house arrest for the last eight years of his life.

Other rigid views of the world included beliefs that deep-sea monsters awaited seagoing vessels to devour them. Giant squids with tentacles miles long could grab a ship and crush it. Along the coast of Africa was a bottomless green swamp where savage beasts were supposed to live. Sailing too close to the equator would cause a sailor's blood to boil. One can see that it took a certain amount of courage to venture off into this uncertain sea of darkness.

However, the atmosphere began to change in the 1500s. Christopher Columbus, followed by other explorers, brought back tales of new and strange lands. More astonishingly, perhaps, they survived the voyages! Expeditions to far-off places seemed less a dream than an actual event.

These new voyages were not so much prompted by a need to know as by a desire for riches—a new and faster route to the treasures of the Far East, including spices, precious jewels, and silks. Over the centuries, caravans traveled the long overland routes through Africa and Asia to bring back the silk finery and exotic spices of the Far East. These were prized items, especially by the wealthy men and women of Europe. But suppose there were a quicker route. Suppose that new world Columbus talked about was actually the Far East, or if not, suppose it was a quicker way to get there. Imagine what that would mean to the country that first found such a profitable route.

A bad beginning

With that thought in mind, European countries, especially England, began the search for the Northwest Passage. One of the first to try was John Cabot.

Cabot moved to Bristol, England with his family, probably in the late 1480s. Records show that he had three sons, Lewis, Sebastian, and Sancio. Sebastian would also gain fame as an explorer. In about 1495, Cabot approached King Henry VII with his idea of a voyage to

14

A reconstruction of Cabot's ship the Mathew *docks in St. John's Harbor, Newfoundland.*

the New World and a search for the Northwest Passage. On March 5, 1496, his request was granted. He would receive financial backing from **merchants** in the port of Bristol. He was to sail "to all parts, countries, and seas of the East, of the West, and of the North" in order to "discover and find whatsoever isles, countries, regions, or provinces of heathens and infidels, in whatsoever part of the world they be, which before this time were unknown to all Christians." It was no small task.

The whole trip started out somewhat badly, however. Cabot's first attempt to sail to North America, in 1496, ended abruptly. He had too little food, terrible weather, and an ill-tempered crew. So he tried again the following May. This time he left Bristol on a small ship, the *Mathew,* with a crew of 20, his son Sebastian included.

It is almost impossible to imagine what life was like aboard the ships of these early explorers. Even by the poor general health and hygiene standards of the time, life at sea was appalling. Roaches and rats were common shipmates on all voyages. All the wooden ships leaked, so water was constantly sloshing around. Bathroom facilities were primitive at best and no one had waterproof clothing. The crew had no regular place to sleep; only the captain and perhaps the pilot got those. The crew slept anywhere on or below deck. The odor was overwhelming.

Food supplies were not much better, especially on the longer voyages. Water and wine casks sprang leaks after a few days of tumbling around. Kegs of grain soon filled with insects. The choice menu of the day was taken from salted fish or meat, rice, onions, cheese, dried peas, vinegar, water, and wine. The only way to get more freshwater on a long trip was to hope it rained.

With the lack of fresh vegetables and poor sanitary conditions, disease was a constant companion on board. About one of five sailors were likely to die of scurvy on a long voyage. This disease is caused by a lack of the vitamin C found in citrus fruits and in fresh vegetables. Scurvy causes the teeth to fall out and the lower legs to become bloated, and may lead to gangrene.

Sailors were highly superstitious and generally religious, too. They offered all kinds of prayers to keep them safe from the elements. They never set sail on a Friday because Jesus Christ was crucified on that day. Some captains held morning and evening prayers at sea, and no sailor was supposed to swear. With all these discomforts and restrictions, it is a small wonder that Cabot or any of the early explorers found enough men to serve on the ships on their journeys.

Cape Race is one of the places that Cabot may have visited in the 1490s.

A landing in North America

On this second voyage, Cabot headed toward Ireland in the *Mathew,* set sail west, and supposedly sighted North America—perhaps Newfoundland—on June 24, 1497. He went ashore and later said that people seemed to be living there because he saw campfire remains and cut trees. However, he saw no one. If he ever met the Boethuks, it might have been later. He did plant the flags of England and Venice to take possession of wherever he was for the English king. After that, he sailed up and down the coastline for a while, naming various spots, such as Cape Discovery, Island of St. John, and England's Cape. Those may have been what today are known as Cape North, St. Paul Island, and Cape Race, all in the area of Cabot **Strait.**

Most scholars think Cabot really did land in Newfoundland. His descriptions fit this land of mostly rocks and ice. King Henry VII named it New Isle. Then it was called "the new founde lande," and finally, Newfoundland.

Cabot then became the first European since the Vikings to reach North America, even if we do not know exactly where. Historians say it was probably Newfoundland, since his descriptions fit, although it could have been southern Labrador, or Cape Breton Island, east of Nova Scotia. Some have said he might even have reached Cape Cod, at the eastern tip of Massachusetts. Satisfied with his discoveries and now deciding that he might possibly have reached the northeast coast of Asia, Cabot headed back across the Atlantic for Ireland.

He crossed the ocean in an amazing fifteen days and was back in Bristol on August 6. That was, by all standards of the time, a speedy voyage. Some doubting historians say it was much too fast; others say the speed might be explained by the fact that most of Cabot's sightings were from his ship.

King Henry had no doubts about anything. He was delighted with the voyage, with the new lands for England, and with Cabot himself. London gave the explorer an enthusiastic welcome. The king gave him a yearly pension and gladly agreed to another voyage.

Cabot's two discoveries

Cabot thought that he had found Asia, possibly the coast of China, on this first voyage. Although he was mistaken, he did report two discoveries that would greatly encourage the development of North America. First, he found the Grand Banks of Newfoundland. This international fishing ground extends for 350 miles (563 kilometers) north to south and 420 miles (676 kilometers) east to west to the south and southeast of Newfoundland. Cabot was the first to report on this incredible gathering of cod, haddock, herring, and mackerel, as well as several types of flatfish. Cold water from the Labrador Current and warm water from the Gulf Stream meet in the Grand Banks. This mingling of

Many sailors believed in sea monsters.

the waters favors the growth of plankton (tiny organisms) and algae that make up the fish food supply.

Once the abundance of fish in the Grand Banks was made public, fishing fleets from England, Spain, France, and Portugal flocked to the area. While the search for a Northwest Passage went on, the fishing fleets operated without much notice. By the mid-20th century, this led to overfishing and to several international disputes. Regulations were needed to protect the fish supply.

Cabot's second find was the Gulf of St. Lawrence. He thought it would lead to China, but later exploration found that it led to the St. Lawrence River.

On Cabot's next voyage, he planned to sail to Japan, a rich source of spices and gems. He was granted permission for this next adventure on February 3, 1498. With five ships and a crew of about 200, without Sebastian, John Cabot left Bristol in May. And to those who still believed the world was flat, he sailed right over the edge. Cabot was never heard from again.

What happened to the explorer, his ships, and his crew? Like much about Cabot's life, no one knows.

Did the voyage meet disaster at sea? Some say the ships reached Newfoundland again, but there is no reliable word on what became of John Cabot himself.

Some historians say that some of the ships might have fallen into the hands of the Spanish. There is at least a little evidence that Alonso de Ojeda, the Spaniard who founded a colony in South America, and Portuguese adventurer Gaspar Corte-Real sailed on later expeditions with some knowledge of earlier discoveries that had been made by the English.

Sebastian also explores

Sebastian Cabot accompanied his father on the first voyage, but he may have destroyed the trip records because of jealousy about his father's fame. After his father's disappearance, Sebastian was a mapmaker in the service of Henry VIII. Because of his skills, he went with the English army to aid the Spanish king, Ferdinand II of Aragon, in their fight against the French in 1512. He was made a captain in the Spanish navy and would have commanded a sea voyage in 1516, but Ferdinand's death cancelled that.

Next, Sebastian worked for Holy Roman Emperor Charles V and gained membership in the Spanish Council of the New Indies. He returned to England in 1520, but was back in the service of Spain in 1525 when he was given charge of a three-ship voyage to the East. He was supposed to have developed trade there. But Sebastian seemed to have other ideas. Instead, he apparently went to explore the Rio de la Plata region of South America. He had heard reports of its great wealth. The three-year expedi-

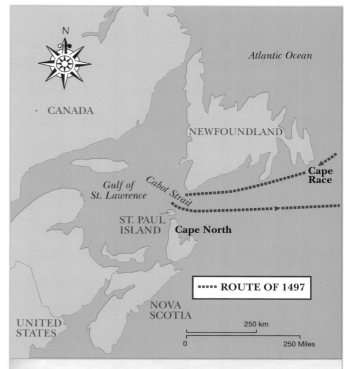

Cabot is thought to have landed in Newfoundland in 1497.

tion was a failure and he was held responsible. He was banished to Africa for two years. Sebastian went back to England in 1548 and, like his father, received a pension from the king. His famous map of the world (1544) is now in the Bibliotheque Nationale in Paris.

Historically, Sebastian Cabot lived in the shadow of his father. The fame of John Cabot was brief and his deeds uncertain. But here and there, especially in parts of Canada, his name is honored as the first European to land in North America since the days of the Vikings.

Chapter Three
Giovanni da Verrazano
Mapping the East Coast (1524–1528)

John Cabot made at least two voyages to the New World. As a result, many places in Canada are named for him. Amerigo Vespucci also made two trips, and he got two continents. Giovanni da Verrazano (also spelled Verrazzano, 1485–1528) traveled to the New World three times. He was the first European to see New York and Narragansett **Bays.** He first saw Block Island and the great harbor of what is now New York City. He journeyed to Brazil, Florida, and the Bahamas. He gave France, for whom he sailed, its claim in the New World. He named many of the things he saw after people and places back in Europe. So why is Verrazano remembered only for a bridge, and one that was not finished until 1964, more than 400 years after his death?

Nevertheless, a splendid bridge it is. The Verrazano-Narrows Bridge, connecting the New York City boroughs of Brooklyn and Staten Island, has a main span of 4,260 feet (1,299 meters). When it opened, it surpassed the Golden Gate Bridge in San Francisco as the world's longest suspension bridge. The roadway of the Verrazano is six lanes wide on two decks. They decks are supported by four cables hung from two towers that are 690 feet (210 meters) high. Verrazano himself might have been impressed.

A drawing of Giovanni da Verrazano (1485–1528)

Most details of Verrazano's life before his first voyage are uncertain. The future explorer was probably born into the wealthy, aristocratic Verrazano family in 1485. That was about seven years before Columbus sailed for the New World. His family's ancestral home was in the Chianti region of Italy, not far from Florence. In fact, Verrazano is usually referred to as a Florentine. Now a noted center of art and culture, Florence was also a great hub of business and politics in centuries past.

The Verrazano-Narrows Bridge stretches from Brooklyn to Staten Island.

Verrazano was well educated for his time and was especially good in mathematics. He also had a love for the sea and decided on a maritime career. So, in 1506 or 1507, he moved to Dieppe, a port in northwestern France. He entered the French service and made several voyages along the Mediterranean coast. Some reports say he made a trip to Newfoundland in 1508.

In 1523, some Italian **merchants** in the French cities of Lyons and Rouen convinced the king, Francis I, to pay for a voyage to the New World. The main purpose was to discover a northern passage to China. By now, the voyage of Ferdinand Magellan (1519–1521) had not only proved that the earth was round, but that America was a separate continent. French ships would also explore the American coast from Florida, claimed by Spain, north to Newfoundland, claimed by England. Between those two points, a mostly unexplored area, they were to find unclaimed land for France. Verrazano would lead the expedition.

In January 1524, Verrazano sailed in the 100-ton (91-metric ton) *La Dauphine*, which he borrowed from the royal French navy. It carried a crew of 50. His brother, Girolamo, a mapmaker, was among them, and his map of 1529 showed his brother's discoveries. There

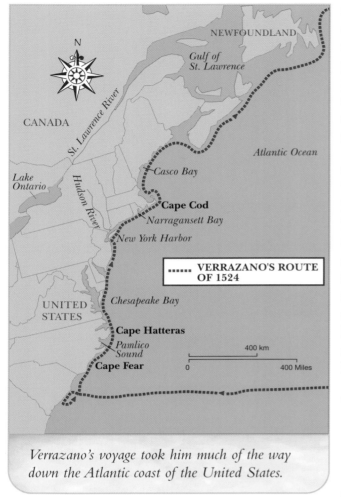

Verrazano's voyage took him much of the way down the Atlantic coast of the United States.

among other items, 1,065 biscuits, 18 dozen loaves of bread, 44 tons (40 metric tons) of flour, 90 chests of lard, 476 pounds (216 kilograms) of butter, 160 pounds (73 kilograms) of candles, and about 12 barrels of water. There was also cider or beer for the crew; wine and fresh meat were for officers only.

Arrival in America

Verrazano set sail west and saw land on March 1, 1524. He was at or near Cape Fear, at the southeastern edge of North Carolina. He sailed south for about another 50 miles (80 kilometers) looking for a harbor. When he could not find one, he turned north again, fearful of getting too close to Spanish claims. As he sailed, Verrazano often gave grand names to what he saw along the shore, but few of his place names stuck.

Verrazano landed near Cape Hatteras. This site is on the Outer Banks, a chain of islands covered with sand dunes that protect the eastern coast of North Carolina from the Atlantic Ocean. From the mast of his ship, Verrazano could see across the banks to a body of water. But he could not see beyond the water. So, he indulged, perhaps, in a little creative—or maybe hopeful—thinking. He exclaimed, "That must be the eastern sea [Pacific Ocean] over there and I must be on the way to China!"

Verrazano was actually looking at Pamlico **Sound,** not the Pacific Ocean. The sound is at most 30 miles (48 kilometers) wide. The Pacific Ocean stretches

is no other record of the crew, although in a later written report Verrazano referred to them as the "maritime mob." That may have been because the crew did not particularly like him. It is said they were given shore leave only once during the entire voyage.

The list of supplies that were needed for a ship voyage in the 1500s is impressive. *La Dauphine* went to sea with, some 12,000 miles (19,312 kilometers) at its widest. Even though Verrazano did not try to reach what he thought was the ocean, the maps of his brother Girolamo, and other maps for quite some time, show North America as a huge continent that tapers to a narrow strip at the coast of North Carolina.

Since the weather was mild and springlike, Verrazano sailed north looking for a way through the narrow land to the Pacific. Some reports say he stopped around present-day Kitty Hawk, North Carolina, where he met Native Americans for the first time and may have kidnapped a child. Probably because he was too far out at sea, he missed the entrances to Chesapeake (between Virginia and Maryland) and Delaware (between Delaware and New Jersey) **Bays.** However, he did sail right into the Upper Bay of New York harbor on April 17, 1524. He was the first European to do so. In his **journal** he called it a "very pleasant place." He also noted some "little steep hills" that ran down into a "great stream of water." That would be the Hudson River, which Verrazano saw before it was "found" by Henry Hudson, for whom it is named.

The largest sound on the east coast of the United States, Pamlico Sound in North Carolina is 80 miles (130 km) long and 15–20 miles (25–50 kilometers) wide.

23

Verrazano anchored his ship in the Narrows. This one-mile-wide strip of water between Long Island and Staten Island was later called the Verrazano Narrows in his honor. Today it is just called the Narrows.

The wind was blowing onshore, so Verrazano pulled anchor the next day and headed north again. After passing Block Island, his next stop was Narragansett **Bay.** Verrazano named one of the islands in the bay Rhode Island after a Greek island of the same shape. Years later when Roger Williams founded his colony, he would keep the name of Rhode Island.

To avoid bad weather, the ship anchored in Newport Harbor and stayed for about two weeks. The crew was able to go ashore for some miles inland, getting as far as present-day Pawtucket. From this period, Verrazano's **journal** provides the first detailed descriptions of Native American peoples, in this case the Narragansett and Wampanoag. He traded with them and said they were "the goodliest people." He also noted that the women in particular were "very handsome" and "as well mannered … as any woman of good education." Verrazano also noted that the land in the region was very fertile and that the native peoples produced the best crops.

Waves crash upon the shore at Narragansett Bay.

But Verrazano was not so taken with the next Native Americans he encountered. Heading north again on about May 5 or 6 of 1525, he sailed through Nantucket **Sound,** around Cape Cod, and up the rugged coast of Maine. Around Casco Bay, near present-day Portland, he met probably the Abnaki or Penobscot tribes. They were much less friendly. Some say that was because they had already come across some European fishing vessels and were not very pleased with Europeans. Verrazano said they were "crude" and had "evil manners." So he named the area "Land of Bad People." He did have much praise, however, for the coast of Maine itself, its natural beauty and "turquoise sea."

Verrazano sailed north again, perhaps as far as Newfoundland, before returning to Dieppe on July 8, 1525. His journal entries provided the first detailed descriptions of people and places in the New World. They were valuable to King Francis because they gave France a claim on the new continent.

A Spanish expedition in 1525 followed Verrazano's route. The Portuguese pilot Estevão Gomes studied the New England coast. An English voyage in 1527, commanded by John Rut, sailed down the Atlantic coast. Both of these trips confirmed Verrazano's findings about the unbroken coast of North America.

Trips farther south

Verrazano was anxious for another trip to the New World. But in 1527, the king could not spare any ships since he was preparing for a war with Italy. Instead, Philippe de Chabot, admiral of France, paid for a voyage to Brazil. Verrazano traveled to the Brazilian coast and returned with a valuable cargo of **logwood,** used for making textiles.

In the spring of 1528, Verrazano was ready to return to the site of his first voyage. He hoped this time to find a route to Asia and he wanted to look south of Cape Fear rather than north. With his brother as a crew member, the ship sailed to the Florida coast and then headed south. Verrazano apparently landed in the island group known as the West Indies. He anchored probably at the island of Guadeloupe. He took a small boat to shore, not knowing that the Carib people were cannibals. As reported by his brother upon the ship's return, Verrazano was killed and eaten by the Caribs.

After his terrible death, the ship continued on to Brazil. The crew picked up another cargo of logwood before returning home with the sad news.

Giovanni da Verrazano's greatest wish was to colonize the "pleasant land" he had found. In his journal he wrote of North America, "We greatly regretted having to leave this region, which seemed so delightful and which we supposed must also contain great riches." He was one of the first to realize that the New World continent was not just a stopping-off point to Asia, but a valuable end of a journey in its own right.

Chapter Four

Martin Frobisher
Looking for the Passage West (1576–1578)

Martin Frobisher (1535–1594) was a most interesting explorer. For one thing, he was born into the English gentry. His uncle was Sir John Yorke, director of the English mint. For another, he was a pirate, or "sea dog"; in the service of the queen to be sure, but a pirate nonetheless. He was also a vice admiral and fought in England's battle against the Spanish **Armada.** He went to the New World three times looking for a Northwest Passage, as well as gold. He did not find either one. He tried to establish a colony in America, but that did not work out. However, he was one of England's most able **navigators** in the Elizabethan age. He was also one of the first Englishmen to search for the Northwest Passage and the first European to chart the waters west of Greenland. Frobisher **Bay** in far northern Canada is named for him. His third expedition into Canada became one of the best-documented voyages of the time, leaving a wealth of information for others to follow. Late in his career, he was knighted for his skill and bravery.

Frobisher was born in about 1535 in the town of Altofts, Yorkshire, England. Little is known about his early years except that his father was well-to-do. However, his father died when the boy was about seven years old. He apparently did not receive much education. There is little evidence that he was

A portrait of Martin Frobisher (1535–1594)

schooled at all, and even in a world where spelling was somewhat lightly regarded, his was dreadful. He seemed to be vague about how his last name should be spelled and often wrote it in several different ways.

One of five children, Martin grew into a big, rebellious teenager. His mother died when he was about fourteen and he was sent to London to live with his uncle. John Yorke was not only master of the royal mint but also a **merchant** adventurer in African voyages.

The term "adventurer" had a somewhat different meaning in Elizabethan times than it does today. An adventurer invested money in outfitting ships for expeditions. Sometimes they actually owned the ships. Sometimes they just supplied the equipment and weapons that would be needed. Sometimes they supplied the goods that might be traded. Sometimes they did all three.

Frobisher stayed with his uncle for about about five years. But what was Yorke to do with a nephew who had no money, no education, and a really bad temper? In the 1500s, the answer was sometimes easy. He was sent to sea.

Actually, that was not generally meant to be a punishment of any kind. Young men often went to sea to improve their lot in life. They could expect to rise through the ranks in the merchant navy. Sometimes they went to learn about the family's trading business. Sometimes they went to sea simply because they thought that farming was very dull.

Very little is known of the next several years of Frobisher's life at sea, but he seems to have made two trading voyages to the coast of West Africa. On one of them, in 1553, he was one of the few survivors. Most of the crew fell ill to a deadly disease called yellow fever. Of 160 seamen who made the journey, only 40 returned.

A trader and a pirate

Frobisher proved to be a skillful and able seaman, daring and resourceful. He began to make a name for himself as a trader and a pirate. Piracy in Elizabethan England operated under a cloak of respectability. Frobisher and other English sea dogs were quietly protected by Queen Elizabeth I. Piracy was, after all, cheaper for the state than maintaining a royal navy. Frobisher and others roamed the waters in search of ships carrying valuable cargo—gold, silks, spices, and even slaves. When the ship returned to port, custom taxes were paid to the crown and Lord High Admiral. Other shares went to outfitters, owners of the ship, and, of course, the captain. Even so, at best piracy was stealing. At worst, it was armed robbery and murder.

Other countries protested the action of the English pirates, Spain in particular. The queen, who did not want to get into a full-scale war, would dutifully bring her "pirates" before the English courts. She could then point out to King Philip II of Spain that piracy was not to be tolerated in England. Usually, however, the pirate was soon on the waters again outfitted with a new ship.

Frobisher rose to the rank of captain about the year 1565. A cold, harsh man, he was strict about discipline and not very popular with those who served under him. But he was popular with the queen. To reward his privateering service, she gave him a ship in 1571 and sent him off to help in England's campaign to subdue Ireland. He kept privateering only as a sideline.

By 1575, England was really getting caught up in the search for a Northwest Passage. Men such as Frobisher and Sir Francis Drake and Captain James Cook would become almost mesmerized by this dream. Somewhere in the great Canadian North, there just had to be a navigable route to the Far East. Surely it was there. Someone just had to find it.

Actually, the Northwest Passage would not be successfully sailed until 1906. Norwegian explorer Roald Amundsen did it in a herring boat called the *Gjoa*. However, it took him three years. In 1944, Sergeant Henry A. Larsen of the Royal Canadian Mounted Police made it in just one season in a **schooner.** While the route of the Northwest Passage is now well known, it is rarely used by commercial ships because is is usually blocked by ice. So it did not become the great waterway that fascinated the early adventurers. Although it dramatically cuts the distances between Europe and Japan, for instance, there are problems of protecting the ships against ice in the Arctic and other complex issues.

But back in 1575, Captain Frobisher had become fascinated with the idea of a passageway to the lands of the East. He had discussed this idea with the knowledgeable Portuguese sailors on his earlier voyages. He knew that French-

An oil painting depicts Queen Elizabeth of England.

man Jacques Cartier had explored as far north as the St. Lawrence River on the American continent. Now he was ready as well.

A first attempt

It took some doing, but Frobisher convinced a group of prominent English citizens to back his expedition. They included Stephen Burrough, who had explored in the Kara Sea north of Russia, and Dr. John Dee, advisor for the Muscovy Company. This London trading group was organized for the express purpose of finding a shorter and more profitable route to trade in the Far East. On June 7, 1576, with high hopes,

Frobisher set sail from Greenwich, England, in command of two light ships, the *Gabriel* and *Michael,* and an even lighter ship known as a **pinnace.** These were rather small vessels by any standards. The biggest of the queen's great ships was 1,000 tons (907 metric tons). The *Gabriel* was 30 tons (27 metric tons), the *Michael* was 25 tons (23 metric tons), and the pinnace only 7 tons (6 metric tons). Even on the Thames River, they must have

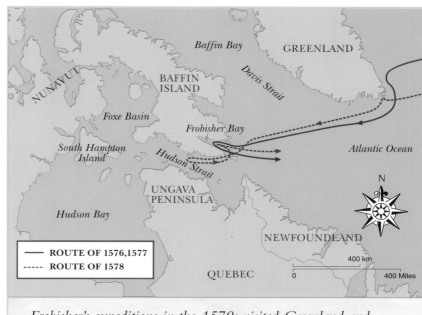

Frobisher's expeditions in the 1570s visited Greenland and Baffin Island.

looked like toys. It is said that Queen Elizabeth waved to Frobisher and his total crew of about 35 as they departed. Kind as this was, Frobisher would have found it kinder if she had decided to invest in the voyage. However, the queen was busy in neverending discord with Spain and at the time wanted no part of risky adventures.

Much more impressive than the ships was the equipment they carried: a book on navigation and a Bible, whose title page had a picture of the queen; a great many of the latest instruments for navigating on the seas; all sorts of compasses and half-hour sand glasses. Frobisher also carried a specially prepared chart. It was a blank piece of parchment with criss-cross lines. The British Isles were

drawn in, and Frobisher was to furnish the rest as he discovered new lands. He did actually draw in some sites around Greenland. Unfortunately, Frobisher also carried a copy of a map from the Zeno brothers of Venice, printed a few years earlier. Supposedly the Zenos had traveled in the North Atlantic in 1380. The map had added false islands, but the English believed it was accurate, which caused navigation problems for many years.

The expedition set sail and went downhill quickly. The pinnace sank in a storm with all hands lost. The other two ships sailed on to Greenland where, at the end of June, the *Michael* just disappeared. Frobisher thought it had sunk. Actually, it had gone home. The captain,

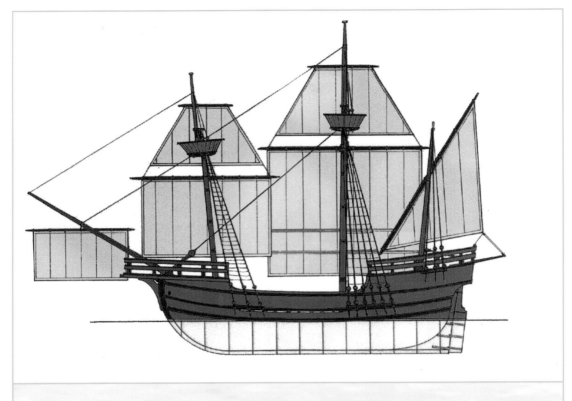

A drawing shows what Frobisher's ships may have looked like.

probably amazed by more ice than he had ever seen, apparently decided the trip was too dangerous and turned back. What had begun as a three-ship expedition was now down to one. The *Gabriel*, commanded by Frobisher, sailed on alone.

By the end of July, Frobisher reached the southern tip of Baffin Island in northern Canada. Convinced that he had at last found the passageway to Asia, he sailed into the **bay** that is now named for him. Exploring the coast, he encountered a group of Native Americans called the Inuit. He thought that the Inuit were trying to indicate the route to follow west, so Frobisher sent five of his men to shore with them. They were never heard from again.

The crew was now down to thirteen. Frobisher thought that the Inuits had kidnapped the men, so he captured an Inuit, thinking they could make an exchange. Nothing happened. With winter closing in, Frobisher had to return to England without his five sailors. He took along the Inuit captive and his kayak.

Frobisher returned to London in October to much admiration. Voyages such as these were very thrilling events in the 1500s. But the center of attention was the Inuit man. Everyone wanted to see this man from another land. Unfortunately, he died in a few weeks, presumably from a cold caught at sea from the sailors.

Besides his hostage, Frobisher returned to England with a collection of plants and one coal-like rock. The black stone was **assayed,** which means to check its content, four times. Unlike the first three assayers, the fourth said it contained gold. Whether he was a fraud or just mistaken is unknown. The stone, however, did not contain gold. It was amphibolite flecked with mica.

Quest for gold

Nevertheless, the gold rush was on. The mere prospect of all that gold made a second voyage assured. Frobisher's personal popularity rose as well. He was promoted to high admiral. And this time, the queen not only contributed money but a ship, the *Aid* (or *Ayde*). The sponsoring group got a royal charter called the Company of Cathay (China).

Ships of the king or queen in the 1500s were something between a personal squadron and a national fleet. The disposal of the ships remained very much a whim of the royal ruler. That is why it was so important for explorers such as Frobisher to gain the monarch's favor. The ships under the ruler's command had names that were kept and passed down for centuries, such as *Rainbow* or *Revenge, Golden Hind* or *Delight*. They were also named for members of the royal family and sometimes, it would seem just for fun, given names like the *Rat* or the *Black Dog*.

The sailors who manned the ships may well have come from generations of seafaring families who lived along the coasts. The ocean was a natural way of life for them. The more adventurous and ambitious, and often the more unruly, were likely to be the ones who were sent on or signed up for the high-risk-taking voyages. The danger was part of the adventure.

On May 31, 1577, High Admiral Frobisher was on his way, this time with the *Gabriel* and *Michael*, both reconditioned, the 200-ton (181-metric-ton) *Aid*, and a crew of about 120. He was told to sail to the region where he had found the black stone and set miners to work collecting the gold. Exploring for a Northwest Passage seemed forgotten. Everyone, even the queen, was caught up in the gold frenzy. No one knows whether Frobisher himself believed that he had found gold. Even if he had thought otherwise, he was unlikely to talk himself out of a second voyage.

Of course, the expedition was a failure because there was no gold and never had been. However, the ships reached the entrance to Frobisher Bay on about July 17. Once in the bay, Frobisher set up headquarters and put the miners to work. They began digging up the black rock. Frobisher really wanted to keep sailing since he was convinced he could sail up the bay to China. But his orders were to stay unless no gold was found. Obviously, the miners were digging up something, and the assayers on board were reporting "a good store of ore." So he waited.

While waiting, Frobisher tried to find out what had happened to the five sailors from the previous voyage. The crew did find some clothes that had belonged to the missing men in a deserted Inuit village. But when some of the Inuit appeared, a fight broke out and several Inuits were killed. The crew took hostages, including an old woman and a mother and her infant. They let the old woman go. Later, Frobisher left a letter with a friendly group of Inuit that promised he would exchange his hostages for the safe return of the men. There was no answer.

By August 21, 1577 the miners had collected 200 tons (181 metric tons) of the black ore and stored it in the ships. Frobisher set sail for England, any exploration now forgotten. On the way home, boredom might have set in, because the

Frobisher Bay in Canada covers an area 150 miles (240 km) long and 20–40 miles (32–64 kilometers) wide.

expedition reported sighting a phantom island, which they called the Island of Buss, somewhere off the southeast coast of Greenland. Besides a name, it was given a shape, some harbors, and a large crowd of whales in its waters. Although no one could ever locate this island, it appeared in John Seller's *Atlas Maritimus* at latitude 57° 30' N. After almost 100 years of reporting this phantom on maps, **cartographers** changed the name to the "Sunken Land of Buss." Then that was finally dropped completely in the 1800s.

Frobisher and crew arrived in London as heroes on October 1. Once again, the hostages, which also included a male Inuit, were the objects of most curiosity. Unfortunately, all three died, probably of European diseases, not long after their arrival in Britain.

Now everyone settled down to await the smelting of the 200 tons (181 metric tons) of ore. At the expected rate of 40 pounds sterling to the ton, the ore would produce 8,000 pounds (3,628 kilograms) of gold. That was more than the entire expedition had cost. It was a fortune! Except, of course, it was not gold.

But like the emperor's new clothes, no one wanted to see that. Although the English assayists kept insisting the ore was not gold, some of the queen's advisors found other assayists who said it was. The pro-gold side won. There would be a third voyage.

Another gold-mining attempt

The Company of Cathay got more money for the expedition. As for High Admiral Frobisher, this time he sailed with a vice admiral and rear admiral under his command, plus the *Aid*, the *Thomas Allen*, 13 other ships, and about 395 men. They included sailors, miners, carpenters, musicians, ministers, surgeons, and colonists. By the standards of the times, this was a huge fleet. The expedition had become a major undertaking. But Frobisher was not going to explore. He was going to bring back gold and establish a colony, leaving about 100 male colonists on the small, barren island of Countess of Warwick (now Kodlunarn). This was the first serious attempt at founding a colony in the North American continent.

Queen Elizabeth I wished Frobisher well, placed a gold chain around his neck, and waved him off on May 31, 1578. The fleet sailed on to Greenland, where the trouble began. In fog that was called a "hideous mist," one of the ships ran into a whale. The *Dennys* was slashed by a mountain of ice. Although the crew was rescued, the ship went down, taking with it the housing in which the colonists were supposed to live. Next, they ran into a storm so bad that one of the crew noted that they were "looking for instant death." As it was, the fleet got lost and instead of entering Frobisher **Bay** as before, the

Icepacks made Frobisher's voyage very difficult.

ships entered Hudson **Strait** to the south. This would have lead them into Hudson **Bay** and probably certain death in the ice. Even though Hudson Bay is to the south of Frobisher Bay, its weather is much harsher.

The crew realized the mistake when the storm cleared, and the ships sailed for Frobisher Bay, which they reached at the end of July. The miners got to work and the Inuit were nowhere in sight, probably not wanting to face such a large assemblage. There was no sign of the missing sailors.

But what about the colony? Most of the housing was gone. The carpenters said they could rebuild it, but it would take two months. It was now August and there was already danger of getting iced in. The decision was up to the captain. Luckily for the 100 colonists, Frobisher made a wise choice for them—forget the colony, finish the mining, and go home. They almost certainly would have died over the winter.

The mining for gold took a month. By that time, tempers were on a short leash. Ice was building. Mild arguments began to sound like **mutiny.** In fact, the pilot of one ship did take over and sail home with the willing crew. Also, there were leaks in the barrels that carried the crew's beer and most of it drained out.

Now it was September 1, and more than 1,100 tons (998 metric tons) of what they hoped was gold were loaded in the ships. Frobisher got the leaders together and asked whether they should go home or explore to the west. The answer was probably a resounding "home," which is what they did. Before they left, the crew built a small stone house on shore. Its remains were found by American explorer Charles Francis Hall about 300 years later.

After another terrible storm, the fleet sailed home without incident. However, Frobisher might well have wished he had gone exploring. In his absence, it had finally been proven that the black ore from the second voyage was not gold, which meant that the ore from the third voyage was worthless, too. Naturally, Frobisher was blamed. The Cathay Company went broke. Some of the crew were not even paid. Everyone blamed everyone else for this disaster. Frobisher's wife was not pleased either. He had married a wealthy widow and invested her money in the Cathay Company.

Frobisher commanded an English ship against the Spanish Armada.

Actually, except for the rift in his marriage, Frobisher did not fare badly. After all, he had not taken part in assaying the black ore. Now at about age 45, he had proved himself an able and skillful seaman and a master of ships. Besides, England needed all its admirals. Still in the queen's good graces, Frobisher helped to put down trouble in Ireland, fighting alongside Sir Walter Raleigh. Then in 1587, he went back to privateering, guarding the English Channel in command of a 25-ship fleet.

In 1588, after years of fighting off and on, King Philip II of Spain decided to invade England with a great "invincible" **armada.** He had about 130 ships, 8,000 seamen, and 19,000 soldiers. The English fleet, under the command of Charles Howard and Sir Francis Drake, defeated the mighty armada in August 1588 and saved England from invasion. During the fighting, Frobisher was in command of the *Triumph*. For his distinguished service, he was knighted by his queen.

Sir Martin Frobisher did not die in battle. He was wounded in the fighting against the Spanish at Brest, France. His wound became infected and he died at home in Plymouth, England, on November 22, 1594.

Chapter Five

Humphrey Gilbert
The Almost Colony (1578–1583)

S ir Humphrey Gilbert (c.1539–1583) was a brilliant man, a creative **navigator,** and a daring soldier. But he was a poor leader. Had he been better, he might have established the first English colony in the New World. As it was, he is credited with claiming Newfoundland for the crown.

Gilbert was born in Devon, England, about 1539, to a family of some wealth. His mother, Katherine, was widowed when he was eight years old. She remarried and Gilbert later became half-brother to Sir Walter Raleigh. He grew up to be the famous English adventurer knighted by Queen Elizabeth I in 1585. That same year another half-brother, naval commander Sir Richard Grenville, carried 100 colonists to what is now Roanoke Island, North Carolina.

At Oxford University, Gilbert studied military science and navigation. An aunt found him a place in the household of then Princess Elizabeth. After she became queen in 1558, she granted him a captain's commission in the army. He was wounded at the battle of Le Havre, France, in 1563. But for some time he had apparently been thinking about a Northwest Passage to the East. In 1566, Gilbert sent a petition to the queen entitled *A Discourse of a Discoverie for a new Passage to Cataia* (meaning Cathay, or China), *Written by Sir Humpfrey Gilbert, Knight*. The last word may have been

Humphrey Gilbert (1539–1583)

wishful thinking or a hint, because Gilbert was not yet a knight. In the discourse he proposed a very ambitious voyage at his "own costs and charges." He would establish English colonies in the New World both for trade purposes and to give jobs to the unemployed. This was enlightened thinking for the time. What Gilbert asked for in return was a monopoly on trade through the passage and a 25 percent cut in taxes charged on goods brought into England.

The queen turned him down. Instead, she sent him off to Ireland where he helped stamp out rebellions in the Ulster and Munster provinces. According to the records, his methods in Munster were very brutal. He also devised an elaborate plan to colonize the provinces. For his services in Ireland, Gilbert was knighted in 1570.

But the queen remained unimpressed about his Northwest Passage scheme. In 1572 she sent him in command of 1,500 English volunteers to aid the Netherlands in a fight against Spain. Here, Gilbert's poor leadership qualities began to show. He constantly quarreled with those in his command and often flew into rages. He also did not win any important battles.

Gilbert returned to England still thinking about the Northwest Passage. But by the mid-1570s, he came up with some other plans, all dealing with North America. He had a plan for England to take over Spain's Newfoundland fishing fleets. He had a plan to occupy Cuba, then held by Spain. And he also had a plan to intercept Spanish ships as they carried silver back to Europe. The queen was still unimpressed.

Whether Elizabeth just grew tired of listening to his many ideas or she

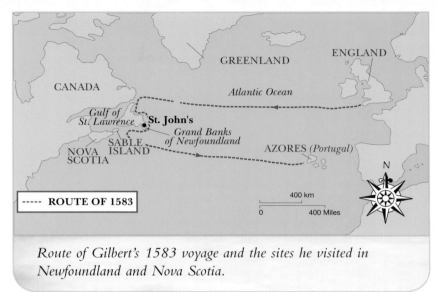

Route of Gilbert's 1583 voyage and the sites he visited in Newfoundland and Nova Scotia.

actually became interested in the plans, she finally gave in. In 1578 Gilbert was granted a six-year charter to settle "heathen lands not actually possessed of any Christian prince or people." Now he had to make good on his promise to supply his "own costs and charges."

A late start

This was not an easy task, even for Gilbert. However, he did manage to outfit seven ships and gather a crew of 365 men. They set sail in late 1578. On paper, the whole expedition looked good. Gilbert sailed in the command ship, the 250-ton *Anne Archer*. All seven vessels were heavily armed and carried provisions for one year.

But the expedition never really got underway. It left on September 26, 1578, already late for such a voyage through the northern seas. The late sailing date might well have been Gilbert's fault. He was always late himself and never quite had the ability to get things done on time. This can be a serious fault in a leader. Not surprisingly, the small fleet was almost immediately struck by fierce storms that sent all seven ships back to port. They tried again on November 19. By that time, however, Gilbert was on bad terms with his second in command, Henry Knollys. In fact, once out at sea, Knollys just sailed off and began raiding ships on his own along the coast of France and Spain. By the following spring, all the ships of the expedition had either drifted back to England or were conducting their own piracy raids along the coasts. Gilbert himself returned to Ireland during the summer to help put down another rebellion.

Yet Gilbert was not easily discouraged. He still had the queen's charter so he organized a second expedition. Raising the money took some time. He was determined not only to find the Northwest Passage, but to establish a permanent colony for England. Toward that end, he signed a document in 1582 providing for a colony to be established even in the event of his death on the voyage. It would be led by a governor and a council of thirteen members. Each immigrant family who agreed to settle in the New World would be given an ax, a saw, a shovel, and some seeds. Church and school would be provided, and all colonizers would have the legal status of English citizens.

Shortly before the expedition was ready, Gilbert heard that the queen did not wish him to go on the voyage. No doubt thinking about his earlier disaster, Elizabeth did not believe he was a very good sailor. But Gilbert immediately sent the queen a letter describing his determination to succeed. Elizabeth thought it over and then wished him well.

Gilbert's second voyage to the New World left Plymouth on June 11, 1583. This time the fleet consisted of about 260 men, including carpenters and stone workers, and five ships. One of the them, the frigate *Squirrel*, was owned by Gilbert. Although it was already getting late in the season for a northern crossing, Gilbert chose that route. He probably wanted to avoid hurricanes to the south. However, he could not avoid the stormy seas. After only two days out, the 200-ton *Raleigh*, owned by Sir Walter, quit the rough waters and went home. The other four ships lost sight of each other in the bad weather. On August 3, when the *Delight*, *Golden Hinde*, and *Swallow* arrived in St. John's, Newfoundland, they found the *Squirrel*, and Sir Humphrey, already at anchor.

Gilbert claimed the island of Newfoundland in the name of Queen Elizabeth I and England. John Cabot may already have done it in 1497, but no one made a record of it, so Gilbert got the honor. A formal claiming ceremony was held in the presence of the crew and about 40 Spanish, Portuguese, French, and English fishermen. The foreigners did not seem to mind that Gilbert was taking the territory for England. The ceremony was held on August 5, 1583, a day still noted by Newfoundland as the birth of the British Empire.

For about two weeks, Gilbert and the crew relaxed and joined in social gatherings with the fishermen. However, there was still a colony to be established, and Gilbert decided to sail south. But the captains of both the *Squirrel* and the *Delight,* by now on bad terms with their captain, said they were ill and refused to go on. Gilbert himself took over the *Squirrel,* put a new captain on the *Delight,*

and set sail with the *Golden Hinde.* The date was August 20.

Gilbert's plan was to investigate all the harbors and creeks along the shoreline to find the ideal spot to establish a colony at Norumbega. This was a name given by mapmakers to an undefined region along the North American coast. But first his fleet of three had to stop at Sable Island off Nova Scotia. Earlier explorers had left cattle there to breed. Gilbert needed fresh meat because he had used up too much of his supplies for the colony while entertaining the fishermen at St. John's.

Explorers would have encountered rough waters, like these in the northern Atlantic Ocean.

Gilbert stopped at Sable Island, Nova Scotia for food and supplies.

Disasters at sea

By August 29, 1853, the small fleet rounded Sable Island. The weather turned bad once again. It was so bad that the *Delight* went down in sight of the other two ships. All of the ship's company, except for twelve men, were lost. The twelve survivors managed to climb aboard a small boat and eventually rowed to the Newfoundland coast where they were rescued.

The crews of the *Squirrel* and the *Golden Hinde* had by now grown upset about the weather and the whole mission. They thought it was too late in the season to be trying to build a colony anyway, especially in such a climate. Gilbert was reluctantly persuaded. "Be content, we have seen enough...."

On August 31, the *Squirrel* and *Golden Hinde* turned homeward. Despite the failure of the mission, Gilbert was in high spirits. He said with conviction that the queen would surely give him the money for two more expeditions.

On September 9, the two ships were hit by a weather front in the Atlantic. Amid the enormous waves, Sir Humphrey Gilbert was seen on the deck of the *Squirrel,* shouting across to the *Golden Hinde,* "We are as near heaven by sea as by land."

Then the little ship with Gilbert and all hands was simply swallowed up by the angry sea. He was 48 years old. The *Hinde,* the last survivor, safely reached the port at Falmouth, England, on September 22, 1583.

Sir Humphrey Gilbert was a strange sort of explorer. He was a sailor not at home on the ocean, a leader without the knack of leadership. He was a man with grand ideas and not quite the know-how to carry them out. But for all that, he served his queen well and gave England a firm footing in North America.

Gilbert stands on the deck of the Squirrel *as it goes down.*

Chapter Six
John Davis
A Path Through the Arctic (1585–1587)

English **navigator** John Davis (also spelled Davys; 1550–1605) was certain he would find the Northwest Passage through the Canadian Arctic. He made three enthusiastic, but fruitless attempts. However, his voyages are interesting and, at the very least, they told future explorers where not to look. They also greatly expanded England's knowledge of the Arctic region. A man of loyalty to his country and his men, Davis was never knighted for his work. He never received any particular honors, and he never received much fame either. But for his tireless efforts, he is regarded today as one of the great Elizabethan sea adventurers.

Part of Davis's lifelong interest in exploring probably came from his friendship with two neighboring seafaring families, the Gilberts and the Raleighs. Like them, Davis was born in the valley of the Dart River in Devon, England. Later in life, he married Faith Fulford, who was related to the Gilberts.

Davis spent some of his young years as a shipmaster. When he was about 33 years old in 1583, he spoke seriously with members of the Gilbert family about a search for the Northwest Passage. He and Adrian Gilbert, younger brother of Sir Humphrey, discussed the idea with John Dee, astrologer and mathematician. Dee often gave advice to navigators who

A drawing of John Davis (1550–1605)

were about to explore the New World. He declared that there were five possible ways to get from Europe to the Far East: two routes that were controlled by Spain and Portugal; a northeast route, which the Muscovy Company had tried and failed to find; a pathway right over the North Pole; and a northwest route. Dee suggested the latter two as being the best choices.

A plan of exploration was given to Sir Francis Walsingham, a secretary to Queen Elizabeth I. So it was that in February 1585, the queen granted a patent to Adrian Gilbert and his associates. They could sail "northwestward, northeastward, or northward." They could take as many ships of any size they wished. They could have a trade monopoly in new lands they discovered. And if they succeeded in planting a colony, they would be given the same powers that had been granted to Humphrey Gilbert.

Being granted a patent for a sailing expedition is one thing, but paying for it is another. Neither Davis nor Gilbert had enough finances to back such a project. So, they called on the **merchants** of London. The merchants responded, and "one Mr. John Davis, a man well grounded in the principles of the art of navigation" was named captain and chief pilot of the expedition. It was a good choice. He was a man of serene disposition, calm in a crisis, and not easily ruffled. He even had kindly feelings toward the native peoples he encountered, a trait often lacking in the early explorers.

Once the money was in, Davis lost little time getting ready. The expedition was not large, even by early standards. It consisted of just two ships: the 50-ton (45-metric ton) *Sunneshine*, with Davis aboard,

Davis spent several years searching for the Northwest Passage.

GREENLAND
Upernavik
Atlantic Ocean
NUNAVUT
Godthaab
Davis Strait
Cumberland Sound
Frobisher Bay
Hudson Strait
UNGAVE PENINSULE
Ungava Bay
Labrador Sea
N
CANADA
NEWFOUNDLAND
----- ROUTE OF 1585,1586
----- ROUTE OF 1587
500 km
0   500 Miles
• Quebec

and the 35-ton (32-metric ton) *Moonshine*, captained by William Bruton. The crew of both totaled 42, which included an orchestra. It seems that no ship could go exploring in the Elizabethan age without musical accompaniment.

Leaving Dartmouth on June 7, 1585, Davis set out on his first search. By July 19, they were in a fog so thick that neither ship could see the other. When the fog broke the next day, they saw the coast of Greenland. It looked so rocky and deserted that Davis gave it a new name, Land of Desolation. The spot was later identified as Cape Discord and appears on maps today as Cape Wallace.

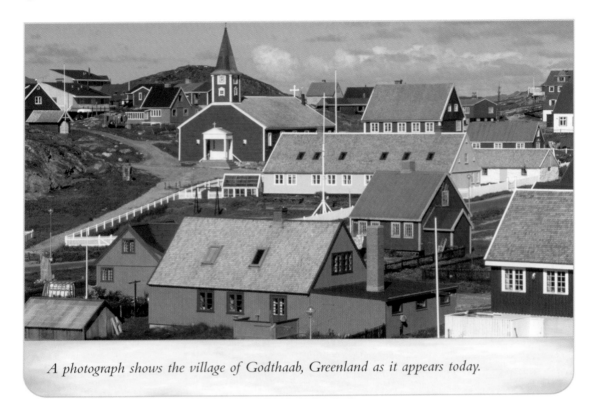

A photograph shows the village of Godthaab, Greenland as it appears today.

Davis, like the other explorers in the northeast at certain times of the year, had to deal with ice forming in the frigid waters. Because it was impossible to break through the ice, Davis sailed south, around the tip of Greenland at Cape Farewell and up the western coast. The small expedition landed at what is now Godthaab. It was there that Davis first met the Inuit, who appeared curious but friendly. To overcome the language barrier, the crew left stockings and gloves on the ground as gifts. But the Inuit were probably most astonished when the ship's orchestra broke into a merry tune and the sailors danced.

The elusive Northwest Passage

By August 1, 1585, with good weather, Davis crossed the **strait** of water that would later be named for him. He headed toward Baffin Island, thinking he was heading toward China. Davis sailed up Cumberland **Sound,** which cuts into Baffin. The water kept getting deeper. The crew sighted whales. The tidal currents grew strong. Surely, this was the way to China.

But now it was August 20. Soon they might be frozen in for the winter, and they had provisions for only six months. With deep regret Davis turned back toward England, where they dropped anchor on September 30. He had not found the passage on his first try, but Davis was not a man to give up easily.

In May he was ready to try again "for the discoverie of the Northwest Passage, in Anno 1586." This time he had four ships: the *Sunneshine* and *Mooneshine* from the first voyage, the *Mermayd,* and the *North Starre*. After one month of sailing, the *Sunneshine* and *North Starre* left the other two, as planned, and headed "straight over the Pole." They were going to test John Dee's idea that the way to the Far East was right over the top of the world.

But not through the ice. Forced to turn back, the two ships stopped at Godthaab on the west coast of Greenland, where Davis had been the year before. They did some trading and socializing with the Inuit.

But the good relations came to a halt when a fight broke out over a Inuit kayak. The result was that three Inuit were killed and a few others wounded, including a crew member.

The two ships turned home. But like Frobisher and Gilbert before them, the mighty sea took its toll. During a fierce storm, the *North Starre* disappeared and was never seen again. *Sunneshine* reached home port on October 6.

Meanwhile, Davis on the *Moonshine* with *Mermayd* reached Greenland on June 15 after a slow sail. Once again, they traded with the Inuit. However, when some of the Inuit insisted on boarding his ship and managed to steal an anchor, Davis lost his temper and sent an armed boat after them. They escaped, but returned the next day apparently wanting a truce. Davis agreed, although he kept one of the Inuit as a hostage. The hostage died shortly thereafter.

Once again, Davis crossed his strait. Once again, he reached Baffin Island. Now he headed south toward Labrador. By early September, however, there were no signs that the Far East was near. Reluctantly, Davis headed his small fleet home, which they reached in October.

Quite amazingly, Davis was not depressed by his two failures. Always optimistic, he declared that the Northwest Passage "must be in one of four places, or else not at all." More amazingly, his financial backers were not depressed and paid for a third voyage.

This voyage left Dartmouth on May 19, 1587, with three ships: the old *Sunneshine,* the smaller *Elizabeth,* and the even smaller *Ellen*. Things got off to a rather poor start. The *Sunneshine* sprung a bad leak after a week at sea, and everything came to a halt while that was located and fixed. Then the Elizabeth had to tow the Ellen while its broken tiller was repaired. After that, Davis had to contend with a near **mutiny.** Some of the crew wanted to sail into a good fishing area right away instead of on the trip home.

With everything straightened out by early June, the fleet was once again at Godthaab. Davis called it Gilbert's Sound. He was also a highly intelligent

navigator who invented many new instruments and gadgets that made sea voyages easier and safer.

On this trip, Davis planned to explore the northern part of Davis **Strait,** now called Baffin **Bay.** But there was more trouble. The *Sunneshine* was leaking again. So, on June 21, Davis let the ship and the *Elizabeth* break away for the fishing grounds. He continued his voyage on the tiny *Ellen.* By the end of the month, he had reached about halfway up the western coast of Greenland into Baffin Bay. This was the northernmost point of his journey. He named it Hope Sanderson for one of the **merchants** who backed his voyage. Today it is called Upernavik.

Turning west and hoping for the lands of the East, Davis ran instead into ice. Pack ice usually blocks this part of Baffin Bay no matter what the season. It took some days to get out of it. Sailing back down Davis Strait past Cumberland **Sound,** Davis missed Hudson Strait, which would have led him into the great Hudson Bay.

Inuits and their dogs stand in front of their igloos.

Ice makes travel through Baffin Bay very dangerous.

John Davis arrived in England on December 15, 1587. His third try for the Northwest Passage was a failure. Yet, Davis had actually found the passage, although he did not know it. Across Baffin Bay from Upernavik is Lancaster Sound. And that is the beginning of the Northwest Passage, finally navigated in 1906. He never knew it, but Davis had found his dream.

The third try marked the end of Davis's northern explorations, although not the end of his career. He was part of England's defeat of the Spanish **Armada** in 1588 and sailed around the coast of South America in 1592. He accompanied Sir Walter Raleigh to the Azores in 1596–1597 and went on expeditions to the East Indies in 1598 and 1601. In 1605, he was killed by Japanese pirates off Bintan Island near Singapore.

Chapter Seven

Henry Hudson
The Four Voyages (1607–1611)

If you travel around northeastern North America, you might think that Englishman Henry Hudson (1565–c.1611) had been everywhere. His name certainly appears in many places. There is the Hudson River, Hudson **Bay,** Hudson **Strait,** Hudson Falls, Hudson Bay Junction, a county in New Jersey, and towns in Massachusetts, Michigan, New Hampshire, New York, North Carolina, and Wisconsin. He also has a bridge and a parkway in New York. Hudson did make four voyages to the New World between 1607 and 1610. Yet, for all that, he is a mysterious man. We do not know where he was born or exactly when. We do not know exactly when he died, where, or how.

Most of what we know for certain about Henry Hudson covers just four years, from his first voyage to his last. These details come from records kept by Hudson and by members of his crew. The rest is filled in from other records, other voyages, and educated guesses.

He was probably born in about 1565 and lived in London. He became a skilled **navigator,** so he might well have gone to school to study his craft. His wife was named Katherine and they had three sons, Oliver, John, and Richard. Several Hudsons were very active in the Muscovy Company of London. In 1585, English navigator John Davis planned a

A portrait of Henry Hudson (1565–1611)

trip to the Arctic while spending some time in the home of Thomas Hudson in London's East End. Perhaps a young Henry Hudson was present at the time. We know that he was well informed about the Arctic and became a very good navigator. The Muscovy Company would sponsor two of his voyages.

Trying a northeastern route

The company had sponsored a number of expeditions with the same disappointing results. However, in 1607 the company decided to try again. So, Henry Hudson in his ship *Hope-well* was sent north to find an ice-free route to Asia. The records of this voyage were published in a book in 1625. With son John, listed as "boy," and a crew of twelve, Hudson sailed from Gravesend, England, on May 1, 1607. After reaching Greenland he turned to the northeast and sailed to Spitsbergen, an island in the Arctic Ocean about 360 miles (579 kilometers) north of Norway. It had first been sighted by Dutch navigator Willem Barents in 1596. In late June Hudson began to explore the island's bays and **sounds.** He did not know it at the time, but he sailed less than 600 miles (966 kilometers) from the North Pole. No one would get closer for a century.

But close was not enough, and the ice was settling in. The storms came and winter in the Arctic was near. Trying in vain to find a way through the ice, Hudson reluctantly gave the order to turn back on July 31, 1607. On the return trip, he sighted Bear Island between Spitsbergen and Norway, and Jan Mayen Island, which Hudson called Hudson's Tutches. Both islands are now part of Norway. A disappointed Hudson and crew returned to the Thames River on September 15, 1607.

Finding himself in the ice-blocked Arctic sea was not only a disappointment but a threat to life and ship. Then as now

icebergs and packs of ice are a real sea-going hazard. An iceberg could easily have destroyed Hudson's small wooden *Hope-well.* It took nerves of steel and a vast knowledge of navigation to avoid these deadly hazards.

Icebergs usually form when the edge of a glacier or icepack splits off in warmer weather. Drifting in the ocean current and the wind, the vast majority of an iceberg is below the surface of the sea. Icebergs vary from about the size of a piano to the size of a ten-story building. Today, sonar and radar keep track of icebergs, and their whereabouts are reported to all shipping in the North Atlantic, sometimes as often as twice a day. A ship's captain in the 21st century is just as worried about icebergs as Hudson was in the 1600s.

Hudson's first voyage was a failure in that it did not find a Northwest Passage and it did not bring profits for the Muscovy Company. But it was not a total loss. He reported many whales off Spitsbergen and walruses around Hudson's Tutches. This sparked the whaling and walrus-hunting industries. Within ten years, they had killed off all the whales and walruses in the area. Today both islands are largely uninhabited and probably look almost the same as they did when Hudson saw them.

Hudson's first voyage also showed that Robert Thorne, an English **merchant,**

The Half Moon *was one of Hudson's ships.*

To the northeast again

Hudson spent the next few months in London waiting for spring. Perhaps he spent his time convincing the Muscovy Company to back another expedition. Either way, on April 22, 1608, he began his second voyage, once again in the *Hope-well* and once again with his son John. This time the crew numbered 15, including four from the first trip.

His mission was the same as before: Find a route to the East through the Arctic. He would sail north, then east, to explore two paths to the Kara Sea north of Russia. Once there, Hudson thought he could sail along the coast of Siberia to China. One route was through the waters north of Novaya Zemlya, a long narrow island. The other route was on a river through the island itself.

The reason for this new sailing plan was a six-foot-long animal tusk. It had been found in the warm waters beyond the Ob River, which flows into the Kara Sea. The tusk was said to be that of a unicorn. This mythical one-horned animal was supposed to live in China. Perhaps the dream of a Northwest Passage was so great that even the slimmest clue was cause for hope. As unlikely as it sounds, the tusk began to be seen as proof that China must be nearby and that a passage to it existed.

At first things looked promising. The sea around Novaya Zemlya seemed to be hospitable. On June 9 the ship's log noted that although the weather was clear, ice was forming. Soon, the ice

was wrong. Thorne very much wanted a successful northern passage for trade purposes. So, he claimed a route over the North Pole was possible because it never gets dark there in summer and because the weather is warm. It is true that at the North and South Poles, day and night are, in theory, six months long. However, these periods are not all light or darkness, but also have twilight. And although the Gulf Stream does moderate the temperature somewhat, it is not warm enough to melt the ice.

floes became so thick and dangerous that Hudson had to turn the ship around and fight his way out. He sailed back to Novaya Zemlya, where some of the crew went ashore, returning with birds and eggs. On July 6, Hudson recorded that the ocean "was so full of ice you would hardly believe it."

Once again, Hudson was forced to turn back. But this time, he had something else in mind. After heading south, he tried to turn the ship toward the west. Historians believe that Hudson was just frustrated with failure. When the route through the northeast was blocked, he was determined to try again for the passage through the northwest.

If that is what he had in mind, it was news to the crew. They refused. Hudson wrote in his log book on August 7, 1608, that he had given his crew "a certificate under my hand, of my free and willing return, without persuasion or force of any one or more of them." If the crew was about to **mutiny,** Hudson might have been forced to sign a certificate absolving them of blame.

The *Hope-well,* a very disappointed Hudson, and a somewhat hostile crew returned to London on August 26, 1608. That may have been Hudson's first mutiny; it would not be his last.

Once again, Hudson had brought back no profits for the Muscovy Company. He did, however, describe the numerous animals and birds he had seen, as well as the large numbers of whales and walruses in the Arctic seas. One of the voyage's most interesting sightings was recorded in the log entry of June 15, 1608. "This morning one of the crew ... saw a mermaid...." He went on to describe a creature with a woman's body, long black hair, and mackerel-like tail fins. Scientists think it likely that the crew was looking at a huge water mammal such as a manatee.

After the second failed expedition, London's interest in a passage to the East via the northeast seemed to cool. Not so in the Netherlands. By the start of the 1600s, the Dutch had become a major sea power and trade network. The Dutch East India Company, or VOC for its initials in Dutch, was formed in 1602. It, too, was looking for a quicker way to the Far East. With about 40 ships, 5,000 sailors, and 600 cannons, the VOC was much larger than the Muscovy Company.

Representatives of the VOC invited Henry Hudson to Amsterdam. This was not unusual. Many explorers sailed under the flag of another country, for example, Italians Christopher Columbus for Spain and Giovanni da Verrazano for France. But when Hudson arrived in the Dutch capital, he found that the VOC was not yet ready to hire him. Perhaps the sponsors had second thoughts about his two disappointing voyages. However, after they learned that Hudson was talking to France about an expedition, they called him back and issued a contract.

Specifically, he was to look *only* for a northeast passage around the north side of Novaya Zemlya. The VOC did not want him to start wandering to the northwest again. It is important to note that Hudson agreed to these terms.

Taking a turn west

Henry Hudson left Amsterdam on his third voyage on March 25, 1609. His crew, English and Dutch, numbered sixteen. Most of the details of this expedition come from the record of one of the sailors, Robert Juet. Only a few scraps of Hudson's **journal** have survived.

This time the ship was the *Half Moon*, forever associated with the explorations of Henry Hudson. It was built in Amsterdam a year earlier and was about 70 feet (21 meters) long. It is difficult to make drawings of ships of that time because the shipbuilders did not use blueprints. In the 1900s, two copies of the *Half Moon* were built in the United States.

The one built in 1909 burned in 1934. The other, built in 1989, is now on the Hudson River at Croton-on-Hudson, New York. It is the home of the Sea Cadets, students who learn the old-time art of sailing under the U.S. Coast Guard. Hudson himself made only one voyage on the *Half Moon*. Historians believe the ship sank in a fight with the British around 1618.

The *Half Moon* sailed up the coast of Norway and before long, there was the old problem of ice and snow. Once again, Hudson turned around. But instead of sailing back to the Netherlands, he turned west—exactly what he had agreed not to do. Neither the records of Hudson nor of Juet report what went on or the reasons for the decision. Maybe Hudson simply was convinced that northwest, not northeast, was the right direction. For whatever reason and whatever the crew's reaction, the *Half Moon* sailed on to the New World. **Navigator** Henry Hudson was to put his name on the map of the world.

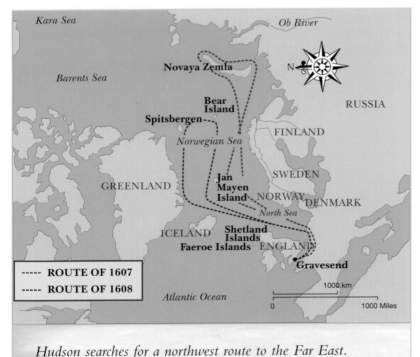

Hudson searches for a northwest route to the Far East.

It was not an easy trip. For a month, the *Half Moon* was battered by terrible storms. One of the masts broke and the sails were in tatters. By mid-July, Nova Scotia was sighted, but Hudson sailed across the Gulf of Maine and anchored off the coast for repairs. During this period, he came in contact with Native Americans who traded with the crew. Although they were friendly and helpful, the ship's log records that upon leaving, the crew robbed them "as they would have done to us." Native Americans soon learned not to be so trustful of these strangers from across the sea. In fact, on this voyage, Hudson and his crew had some unfriendly encounters with the native peoples.

Once the repairs were completed, Hudson sailed south to Cape Cod, Massachusetts, and then all the way down the coast to Virginia and Chesapeake **Bay.** Why would he head south if he was looking for a Northwest Passage? Some months earlier, Captain John Smith of the Virginia colony at Jamestown had told Hudson that a river north of that site might be a way to the western sea (the Pacific). Hudson actually passed the entrance to the James River (then called the King's River) where Smith's colony was located. He probably did not stop to see his old friend because he was flying Dutch colors and did not want to be mistaken for an enemy. By August 24 the *Half Moon* had reached Cape Hatteras, North Carolina, but severe storms caused Hudson to turn north.

The ship entered Delaware Bay in late August. Hudson probably saw what is now Cape May at the tip of New Jersey, and then began to sail up the Delaware River between New Jersey and Delaware. Soon, however, he realized that this was not the the river that would take him to China.

Back down the river and north again, on September 9, 1609, Hudson and the *Half Moon* were at the entrance to the beautiful river in New York harbor that bears his name. It is this part of his journey that brought him lasting fame and so many places with his name on North American maps.

For the next month, Hudson's journal details what he called "as pleasant a land as one need tread upon." He wrote of the excellent harbor, of the beauty of the scenery as they sailed upriver, of the abundance of forests, and the friendliness of the native peoples. However, he also records instances of meetings that were hostile. One of the crew and a number of Native Americans were killed in an encounter. Some six years after Hudson's exploration of the mouth of the Hudson River, the Dutch government would build a fort there. And in 1625, the town of New Amsterdam would be founded on the site of what is now New York City.

By September 16, 1609, the *Half Moon* had sailed up river to about the site of Albany, New York. Although the journey was pleasant, Hudson must have realized by now that this was not the way to the Far East either. On September 22 the water was too shallow to go farther, so Hudson turned around again. On the way back, they passed imposing white-green cliffs. These are sandstone bluffs known as the palisades, from 200 to 540 feet (61 to 165 meters) high, on the west side of the Hudson River across from a green island that the Native Americans called *Manna-hata*. That is now the island of Manhattan, the heart of New York City.

Hudson left his river on October 4, and arrived in England on November 7. Why did he not return to Amsterdam? Several reasons have been given. Supplies were running out. The English part of the crew insisted. Some believe that a **mutiny** took place during the early days of the voyage when the Dutch crew rebelled against the ice and snow. They might have feared punishment on returning to the Netherlands. Hudson

An oil painting depicts the eastern harbor of Amsterdam as it appeared in the 1600s.

was also not anxious to see Amsterdam after disobeying his contract.

Once in London, Hudson and his crew were not allowed to go to Amsterdam to report on the voyage. In fact, Hudson was not allowed to sail again for the Dutch. The British had become irritated with Hudson's willingness to sail under the Dutch flag. He was England's most famous **navigator,** and the British had no intention of letting even more glory fall to their rivals because of his voyages. So, Hudson gave his report to the Dutch consul in London. In addition, the British did not return the *Half Moon* to its rightful owners in the Netherlands until Hudson had left on his fourth voyage. The crown was taking no chances.

To the northwest this time

The fourth voyage of Henry Hudson was his last … and most mysterious. Very little of his **journal** about this trip remains. It begins on April 17, 1610, and ends abruptly on August 3—the end of journal and apparently end of Henry Hudson. Another journal from crew member Abacuck Prickett provides more details.

This time Hudson was backed by an independent group of five noblemen and thirteen London **merchants.** He was authorized to find a Northwest Passage. And this time he got a bigger ship to command. It was the 55-ton *Discovery,* carrying a crew of 22, including Robert Juet from voyage three,

possibly four others who had sailed with Hudson, and once again, his now teenage son John.

If Hudson had learned anything on his previous expeditions, it was that the Northwest Passage was not along the eastern seaboard of America. It had to be through one of the **straits** in the Canadian Arctic. So Hudson sailed toward Greenland and then southwest. He was looking for what was described in an earlier voyage by English explorer George Weymouth as a "furious overfall" of water. This seemed to suggest a great body of water behind it. Hudson was sure it was the Pacific Ocean.

Alas for Hudson, what lay behind the "furious overfall" was the huge **bay** in northern Canada that bears his name. Once in the bay, he followed the coast south and then west. Eventually, he found himself at the southernmost point of Hudson Bay, called James Bay. He sailed around somewhat aimlessly, with no outlet to the Pacific and winter in the Arctic coming on.

The situation was destined for trouble. The *Discovery* had to winter in James Bay. The ice was treacherous. The crew hauled the boat aground and built a temporary shelter. The ice and bitter cold were severe. Sailors suffered frostbite and lack of food. Hudson had hoped to come in contact with Native Americans for food and supplies, but that failed. With no way to get fruits and vegetables, the crew developed scurvy, caused by lack of vitamin C in the diet.

This reconstruction of Half-Moon, *built in 1989, is now on Hudson River at Croton-on-Hudson, New York.*

Their gums turned black and their teeth fell out. Their joints became swollen and some could no longer walk. Members of the crew thought Hudson was secretly keeping food for his favorites. In addition, Hudson had demoted Juet for behavior he did not like. This prompted Juet to side with those whose dissatisfaction with the captain was growing. And although Hudson told his men that they would return to England as soon as the ice freed the ship, the crew was suspicious that he would continue sailing west.

In mid-June the *Discovery* was still locked in the ice of James **Bay.** What had become louder and louder grumblings among the crew now turned into a full-fledged **mutiny,** which most likely involved Juet. This was not an action to be taken lightly. At the time mutiny was the most severe of crimes, punishable with death by hanging. That is because it was believed that the safety of a ship depended upon each sailor's full obedience to the captain. Today mutiny is rarely heard of, but it is still regarded as a very serious offense, punishable by a court martial.

And so it was that on June 22, 1611, some crew members of the *Half Moon* rebelled. Others would have nothing to do with what they knew was a hanging offense. The mutineers tied up Hudson, his son, and six sailors who were sick. They put them in a small open boat along with a gun, some grain, an iron pot, and some spears. The ship's carpenter, Philip

Staffe, asked to go along with Hudson, who was his friend. These nine were set adrift in Hudson Bay.

No one knows what happened to the great **navigator,** although it is logical to assume that nine men in a small open boat in the frozen Arctic did not stand much of a chance. Henry Hudson was never heard from again, nor were the other eight. About 20 years later, the ruins of a small shelter were found on the bay shore. It was possibly erected by the castaways.

In July, the remaining sailors tried to trade with Native Americans. The mutiny ringleaders were killed in a fight with them. The *Discovery* set sail for England. This was not an easy task with nine men gone from the crew and food supplies very low. The survivors were reduced to eating candle wax by the time the ship reached England. Robert Juet died of starvation aboard ship. Of the thirteen men who left Hudson Bay after the mutiny, only seven stepped ashore on English soil.

Naturally, the survivors all blamed the dead sailors for the mutiny. Strangely enough, it took five years for the crews to be brought before the court to testify. Ship's mate Robert Bylot was pardoned since he had brought back the ship. The charges were dismissed against the others. It seems that the sponsors were more interested in what had been learned about a Northwest Passage than in what had happened aboard ship.

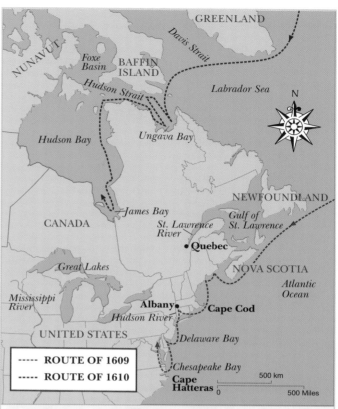

Hudson visited a number of sites along the coasts of what would become the United States and Canada.

Looking for Hudson

Two years after Hudson disappeared, the *Discovery* and the *Resolution* were sent back to Hudson Bay. They did not have Hudson's **journal,** but they had his map. Many still believed that he had found the Northwest Passage. Five men died on this voyage. There was no trace of Hudson or the other castaways. The expedition proved that the huge **bay** had a western shore and it did not lead to the Pacific Ocean. In 1616, the *Discovery* went back, this time with Robert Bylot as captain. He returned convinced that this was not the route to the Far East.

Looking over his four voyages, it might seem that Henry Hudson, for all his fame, was a failure. He did not find what he most sought—a Northwest Passage. He charted no new sea routes and discovered no new continents. His leadership was questionable. He was indecisive at James Bay. He certainly was not a great judge of shipmates. Juet was a troublemaker and often drunk, which Hudson knew from the start. He broke his contract with the Dutch. And at times he appeared more pigheaded than courageous.

But overall, the four voyages of this splendid **navigator** contributed much to the world's knowledge. He brought his crews through dangerous Arctic winters and added to the explorations of such adventurers as Verrazano and Gilbert. He explored the northern reaches of the globe in all directions, sailing through treacherous ice, biting cold, and vicious winds. He contributed greatly to mapmaking and to knowledge of the North American continent. He gave England the right to claim much of Canada. And he gave the Netherlands a claim to a large chunk of the New World. Dutch colonies began to grow, especially from New York to Delaware, and Dutch influence lasted into the 1600s.

Hudson is rightly remembered for all those things. Mostly, however, he is remembered today for doing what the

A mutinous crew forces Hudson off his ship.

early explorers were supposed to do. Any list of those who changed and expanded our knowledge of the world must include the adventurous English navigator Henry Hudson.

What Did They Find?

Between the days of Leif Ericson and the last voyage of Henry Hudson, from about the year 1000 to the year 1611, the world grew vastly larger, at least in the eyes of the Europeans. Year by year, decade by decade, explorers set out to discover what was over the horizon or around the next bend. All of them faced danger and many of them failed. They did not navigate a Northwest Passage, as many of them hoped to do. They did not build new colonies in the places they had found. They lost ships and crews and money and sometimes even their lives.

Yet, each of the seven explorers in this book won something. And even more, each of them left something to those who followed. Leif Ericson went home to Greenland with tales of a new land to the west. Nearly 500 years later, Cabot landed there and spread English names around the New World. Verrazano returned to Europe with wondrous tales of magnificent harbors and a strange but mostly friendly people who lived there. Frobisher began to open the Canadian northeast in his fruitless attempts to find the passage west. Gilbert also failed to start a colony but was able to claim Newfoundland for England. Davis did not actually find the Northwest Passage, but his failures showed others where not to go. Henry Hudson led the way to the New World. His explorations would eventually lead to some Dutch influence and more English colonies in what became the United States.

The story of these seven adventurers is an exciting story of change. Changing things are what explorers do best.

Important Events in the Exploration of Northeastern America

c. 1000   Leif Ericson sails to the northeastern coast of North America, perhaps to Newfoundland or Nova Scotia

c. 1011   Icelander Thorfinn Karlsefni unsuccessfully attempts a colony on Greenland

1497   First voyage of John Cabot, possibly to Newfoundland

1498   Cabot's second voyage; disappears without a trace

1524   Giovanni da Verrazano's first voyage; sails U.S. coast, enters Upper **Bay** of New York harbor

1528   Verrazano sails to West Indies; captured and eaten by Caribs

1576   Martin Frobisher sails to Baffin Island in northern Canada

1577   Frobisher's second voyage, to Frobisher Bay

1578   Frobisher's third voyage, to Frobisher Bay

1578   Humphrey Gilbert receives 6-year charter to colonize; first expedition a failure

1583   Gilbert claims Newfoundland for England, sails to Nova Scotia and Sable Island; disappears on voyage home

1584   John Davis sails to Greenland, Davis Strait

1585   Davis sails to Greenland, Baffin Island

1586   Davis's third voyage, to Baffin Bay

1607   Henry Hudson sails to Greenland, Spitsbergen

1608   Hudson's second voyage, northeast to the Kara Sea

1609   Hudson reaches U.S. coast, Maine, Cape Cod, and Virginia; sails up Hudson River to Albany

1610   Hudson's fourth voyage, to Hudson Bay

1611   Hudson is set adrift in a **mutiny,** and disappears

Major Dates in the Search for the Northwest Passage

1496–98 Voyages of John Cabot; disappears on second expedition

1576–78 Voyages of Martin Frobisher

1585–87 Voyages of John Davis

1611 Henry Hudson sails into Hudson **Bay** in *Discovery;* never heard from again

1612–15 Robert Bylot and Thomas Button in *Discovery* search Hudson **Strait**

1616 Bylot and William Baffin in *Discovery* sail beyond Upernavick

1670 Hudson's Bay Company established; several unsuccessful attempts to get through from Hudson Bay

1753–54 Ben Franklin promotes expedition by Charles Swaine in the *Argo*

1819–22 First expedition of Sir John Franklin, to King William Island, Canada

1819–20 Sir William Parry reaches Melville Island through Lancaster **Sound** in the *Hecla*

1829–31 John and Sir James Clark Ross in *Victory* reach Boothia peninsula, Canada

1845–48 John Franklin's second expedition, in *Erebus* and *Terror,* last seen at entrance to Lancaster Sound; all perish

1850–54 Robert McClure, H.M.S. *Enterprise,* travels passage west to east but partly on foot

1903–06 Roald Amundsen, in fishing sloop *Gjoa,* completes first passage

1940–44 Henry A. Larsen of the Canadian Mounted Police completes first two-way passage in *St. Roch*

1954 *Labrador,* Canadian icebreaker, completes passage

1957 *Storis, Spar,* and *Bramble,* U. S. Coast Guard cutters, complete passage with the aid of icebreakers

1958–60 U.S. submarines *Nautilus, Skate,* and *Seadragon* complete passage underwater

1969 Tanker *Manhattan* for Standard Oil of New Jersey completes passage

The long-sought Northwest Passage, although technically solved, has never become a short, commercially profitable route from Europe to the lands of the East.

Glossary

armada large force of moving things, such as fishing boats; in the days of the early explorers, often used to designate military force of a nation

assay examination of characteristics (e.g., weight or quality), such as in a gold assay

artifact a human-made item, usually a tool or ornament, that represents a culture or a particular time

bay small body of water set off from the main body, such as Delaware Bay is set off from the Atlantic Ocean

cartographer one who makes maps

journal a record of events, such as a day-to-day log of a ship's voyage

logwood hard, brown wood found in Central and South America; often used for dyes

merchant term generally in use in earlier centuries for a person who ran a business

mutiny revolt against superior officer, as by a ship's crew

navigator one skilled in methods of determining a ship's course and position on an ocean voyage.

pinnace light sailing ship

prow pointed bow, or front, part of a ship

saga long, detailed heroic narrative; some were recorded in Iceland in the 1100s and 1200s

schooner sailing vessel, usually two-masted

sound long inlet of water usually parallel to the coast

strait generally narrow passageway of water connecting two large bodies of water

Further Reading

Bohlander, Richard E., ed. *World Explorers and Discoverers*. Cambridge, Mass.: De Capo, 1998.

Goodman, Joan Elizabeth. *Beyond the Sea of Ice: The Voyages of Henry Hudson*. New York: Mikaya, 1999.

Healy, Nick. *Giovanni Da Verrazano*. Minneapolis: Lake Street, 2003.

Johnson, Donald S. *Charting the Sea of Darkness: The Four Voyages of Henry Hudson*. New York: Kodansha, 1996.

McDermott, James. *Martin Frobisher, Elizabethan Privateer*. New Haven, Conn.: Yale University Press, 2001.

Riendeau, Roger. *A Brief History of Canada*. New York: Facts on File, 2000.

Shields, Charles J. *John Cabot and the Rediscovery of North America*. Broomall, Pa.: Chelsea House, 2001.

Index